By: A Jean White-Jennings
Copyright 2013 © A Jean White-Jennings

All rights reserved. This book is protected under the copyright laws of the United States of America. This book may not be copied or reprinted for commercial gain or profit. The use of the historical background is public domain information and used only as an example for personal growth and to encourage personal development. Permission will be granted upon request for copying for use as a personal group study guide. Unless otherwise identified, scripture quotations are from the Kings James bible.

29:11

Everyone's Foundation for A Success Filled Life!

This book is based on a portion of the public lives of Sam Cooke, Teddy Pendergrass, Whitney Houston and Donna Summers for illustration purposes of how we can overlook our spiritual wellbeing in the midst of our success. For individual insights for Sam Cooke TruTV; for Teddy Pendergrass his Official web page and insights from various news articles; for Whitney Houston, her Official Site and for Donna Summers her Official site.

ISBN: 978-0-9825851-1-5
For Worldwide Distribution
Printed in the U.S.A.

Table of Contents

Dedications — i
Acknowledgements — ii
Introduction — iii

Chapter 1: Sam Cooke

Chapter 2: Teddy Pendergrass

Chapter 3: Whitney Houston

Chapter 4: Caught Up In the Hype

Chapter 5: Deceived

Chapter 6: Another example of Deceived Only For a While; then She Remember God

Conclusion

About the Author

DEDICATION

This book is dedicated to all the precious people of God who may be struggling or who may know of someone who is struggling with how to utilize their skills to honor God. They are caught between using their gifts and talents to get closer to God or to obtain monetary wealth.

It is also dedicated to Elder Luther and Mother Doreatha Edwards, of Illinois, whose words of encouragement have helped to keep me focused and unafraid to use my God given skills. I am so sad that Mother transitioned before 29:11 was completed.

Also to my beloved son, Matthew Jennings who before his transition was instrumental in helping me to learn the true meaning of unconditional, everlasting love.

To my Grandmother, Mary Lee Evans, who was the epitome of excellence as a mother, a grandmother and friend.

And lastly to those family members who have always supported and encouraged me to keep going in my quest to fulfill my dreams; my nephews Arnold, Daniel and Ellis; my cousin Valeria; my sister-in-law Wilma and to the entire Winkfield, Motley, and Williams family, who for the past forty-plus years have been my only family; to my Sisters, Melody and Kim and my brother Anthony. Last but not least to my Georgia family the Combs, thank you for loving me in spite of everyone else; and the White Family of Fayetteville Georgia.

ACKNOWLEDGEMENTS

To Pastor Lovie Nichols who never ceases to teach me as well as others through her actions and support. She truly gives meaning to the age old adage; actions speak louder than words.

A special thanks to countless others who have impacted my life both naturally and spiritually, you know who you are. To Yolanda Wilson and Valeda Williams – the movie is coming.

Special, special thanks goes out to a quiet, soft spoken woman who is the example of what a wife should be; Anna Hannah, wife to Pastor John Hannah of New Life Covenant Church South East, Chicago Illinois. Thanks Pastor for being who you are in the Lord.

Thanks you to my Grandchildren, Branden and Spairo who always let me know they love me and that their Mamo (me), rocks.

Lastly, I wish to give special thanks to my friends; the Walkers. They have given me their support, friendship and love as they encouraged me to pursue my passion for writing.

INTRODUCTION

29:11 – Everyone's Foundation for A Success Filled Life

For I know the thoughts that I think toward you, saith the LORD, thoughts of peace, and not of evil, to give you an expected end. (Jer. 29:11)

Webster defines the word "discover" to mean the first person to find or learn something previously unknown; to find somebody or something unexpectedly or after a search. It also defines "expected" to mean "await" to anticipate or look forward to the coming or occurrence of.

The word "discovered" has troubled me since I was a grammar school student. The definition of the word has many variables, all of which lead back to someone or something to be the first to learn something about or; to identify someone for the first time. When historians stated that America was discovered I had difficulty wrapping my brain around that concept. As a grammar school student for historians to claim they had discovered America was hard for me to conceive since people were already living on this continent.

As a result, viewing things from a child's perspective, after hearing this part of history, I lived in fear of someone coming to my father's house and claiming it, stating they "had discovered it" much like the settlers did with this continent; a country which was already occupied? But that's another story.

That was in the natural. However, when I reference the word "discover" in the bible, it seems to refer to man's inability to discover something.

When the bible refers to a place it clearly acknowledges nations or tribes who occupied the land before others arrival. No matter what beliefs, talents, or abilities the people who lived in a place had, they were acknowledged.

No matter where you go you will always find men and women doing what they are gifted to do. Whether it is in the music field, sports, speaking; no matter what it is you can believe if that person is outstanding in a subject it is their gift. When it comes to man's ability to know the mind or the thoughts of God, the bible states repeatedly that man does not know the thoughts of God. Man cannot discover anything about his future. (Ecces.7:14) Unfortunately, there is always someone who comes along and acts under the premise of discovering someone else's talents, abilities and gifts or even claiming to have discovered the person themselves. How can the so-called "discovered" be so blind in their excitement of being recognized? We are all too often so easily deceived. Dangle a dollar or a trinket under our noise and off we go. Those that claim to have discovered or found someone bases their findings on them seeing people using their God given gifts for the first time. According to the word of God, every good and perfect gift comes from God. (James 1:17) Every good gift and every perfect gift is from above, and comes down from the Father of lights, with whom is no variableness, neither shadow of turning.)

If God provides us with our many gifts and talents why do we allow others who lack our skills and abilities or whose abilities are questionable to take and use our God-given gifts and talents to gain wealth? Talented people rely on others with questionable integrity; people, who are great manipulators; who convinces us that they have our best interest at heart for guidance; when in fact it is their own interest; money that can be made in their eyes through the exploitation of others.

Allow me to share with you some artist whose careers and talents I have admired for years and continue to admire to this day. These icons immediately came to mind because they each shared a common thread, their initial love for God, along with their exceptional talent. I am sure you can name a few of your own. Each of these greats is renowned; all were spotted doing what they had been gifted to do; fulfilling their destiny. I selected them because they are among my personal favorites. These icons cover three career generations; their fates were the same, self destruction; and at some point they all depended on some form of artificial stimulant to cope. They were dependent on drugs, alcohol or a personal relationship that was toxic. Perhaps you can think of others, or someone you may know personally who fits into this group quite well.

Each had their own unique abilities; each had their own personal battles to overcome, while the world's traps, tricks and schemes aided in their destruction.

It is my desire that this book can serve as an illustrated source that upcoming artist can use as a guide to success.

They were great men and women who fell into the traps of the trade, which brought them, what I believe to an early death.

My selection crosses three generations; my father's, mine and my children's. As we look at the destruction of these greats it can provide us with an opportunity to learn and grow. But will we grow or will we take the posture of it won't and can't happen to me or mine?

I would say they failed to grow at all. We think what happened to them won't happen to us as we sell our gifts for the benefit and gain to others? Our divided share of the wealth pie is just enough to make us think we are getting our fair share. However, many times in the end we end up penniless while our benefactors are rich beyond means?

If we take the time to learn the Creator of our gifts, we will be wealthy beyond our imagination; that is what the word says; more than we can even imagine or think (Ephesians 3:20); promotion comes from the Lord (Ps 75:6-7); need I say more?. We seek the approval of man more than the Creator. We take so much for granted, but in the end if we are reckless and we fail to do the right thing we embark down paths of self destruction, never realizing we have strayed off our path.

You may think that because I have selected people from the secular arena I am criticizing them but you would be wrong.

The fact is it is those that are in the secular arena who started in the church that the enemy seeks to destroy first.

However, that does not mean that he has not set his sight on those of us who remain in the house. The devil wants us even more than those he has lured away, he has them already. The devil is cunning; he attacks the saints in various ways. Gifted artist whose beginning started in the church are the ones; satan set his traps on so they can fall. He uses his tricks and traps to stand and accuse us before God. (Job 1:7)

But he is so dumb. Satan's prey may have fallen for the trap but it does not mean their souls and hearts turned from God. The artists that are in the secular arena that were pulled from the church are the ones who appear to fall the hardest. The fact is some gospel artists who have not strayed from the house, do themselves more spiritual harm than the artist who has been pulled from the church. They present stumbling blocks for the people, who look to them as role models. Some soul could be lost as a result of their behavior. It's been my experience in areas where I have resided and worked with promoters, when it comes to working with secular artist verses gospel artist, most promoters would much rather work with secular artist than gospel artist. This is not to say that all gospel artist have bad reputations, it simple says that in the gospel arena we should be an example and not looked upon as the problem. Satan attacks the minds of promising artist making them believe they are greater than they are, because satan recognizes the hand of God is on their life.

There are a great number of secular artist who have the respect and hearts of their followers more than followers of gospel artist. Secular artist appear to love their followers; some set better moral examples for their supporters to follow than some gospel artist. Some gospel artists have attitudes and body language that sends a negative signal which says; "I am unapproachable." Secular artist fans, collect their music; while gospel artist fans, listen and move on.

In my role as a radio announcer I have witnessed firsthand the attitudes of what we in the industry call the "one CD wonders", verses industry greats on the secular side; as well as some top billboard artist; both gospel and secular, and it never cease to amaze me that those who have the least seem to act the worst. Sometimes it is the reverse, but seldom is it artist who have recognized successes that are difficult to work with according to promoters. There should be a mandatory training created to teach promising artist how to conduct themselves. The bible warns us to be careful of how we entertain strangers. (Heb. 13:2) With that in mind, the same principal applies in our daily walk as Christians we never know who we are meeting. Often it is obvious that many of the new stars are very talented, it is their character many-times that prevent or hinder their success. I have often heard that God does not take you where your character can't keep you.

So ask yourself if you know a promising star, did God lead them to where they are or did Aunt Sadie tell them they could sing and they ran with it?

Do they actually have talent and lack character; or are they still babes seeking directions? God does not create messes. Many promising stars spend their time and energy working their local markets in an effort to make a name, all the while demonstrating nasty attitude which they don't see as the reason for them not succeeding. The word says your gift will make room for you (Prov. 18:6). Are they gifted? Their explanation for them not succeeding is they perceive others are jealous; which is what the new artist claims is holding them back. The fact is they are holding themselves back. They lack mature talent and character; if the truth be told no one wants to be associated with someone when they are out of control.

Sometimes the artist realizes their actions have cut their career potential. When they realize they need to make a change they sometimes move on. After relocating they don't always remain the same person they were.
They learned through their failures or someone loved them enough to tell them the truth about themselves to help them on their path to success. There are highly gifted, anointed and dedicated people who just never seem to take the right path as a result they never live up to their true potential.

Let's acknowledge there are a significant number of artist who are known because they have written many great songs or they were once part of a famous choir. These unsung greats past and present realized they are examples and that is how they lived their lives. Not all are held back because of a bad attitude.

For some their season has not come and God has them right where He wants them.

I have lived in many places throughout the US, and have been favored to be in the presence of some great men and women. Guess what when it comes to being high minded, I have found the truly greats are not high minded. I mean they speak whenever they see you; they are not puffed up; they are not proud; they do not seek their own. It sounds like these artists are doing it God's way. They are successful in their own right. These song-birds, writers, musicians and even some sports legends are always the same no matter where you see them.

I know like everyone else in this world, they have problems, they are sometimes over-looked and forgotten, their talents have been exploited yet they still choose to love and trust God, even if they don't openly profess their faith. To tell you the truth not all of them are gospel artist, many are cross-over and even some are secular artist. Then there are those that think because they have a family name that is synonymous with gospel they are grand.

Allow me to explain; I worked an event where a world famous mother and daughter act in the gospel arena were part of the program. It was a summer festival in the park and the daughter arrived early in the day with about 20 people. This group was rude and felt they should receive preferential treatment. When the mother finally arrived, she rode up to the stage in her vehicle sang her song, got back in her car and rode off.

As mentioned this was a summer park event which meant interacting with the attendees. This was not the case with this artist. Looking back, it was easy to see where the daughter had gotten her attitude; the apple never falls far from the tree. Nothing about their character was Christ like, they were rude and they did not set an example for others to follow. When we serve as God's representative, we must be mindful of our words, deeds and actions.

Many of the attendees had sat in the hot sun most of the day, so they could have a good seat when the artists ministered. This artist blew their opportunity to reach some lost soul by failing to reach out to the people.

When such negative behavior is known it can and does hinder and throw stumbling blocks in the pathway of non-believing followers; whether it is in the music arena, the pulpit or the sports arena. There are some things that should not be. It is a good feeling when I sometimes leave home, and some of the neighboring children ask, "You going to church?" I find this funny because, I don't walk around with a bible in my hands nor do I stand on my porch and preach, I do however, allow my lifestyle to speak for me.
There are countless, athletes, preachers, teachers, singers, musicians and such who allow their lives to speak for them and of their beliefs. There are far too many to name them. By no means am I bashing those I have chosen to highlight. On the contrary, I recognize the devil deceived them and it is my hope that others will see the works of the enemy and this will keep them from falling into the same trap.

I truly believe the devil tricked them. They were tricked out of their place of honor to follow a promise they were destined to receive without the help of the trickster because it was their destiny. So as we step into the shadows of several gifted people whose hunt for fame came at a price they were not prepared to pay, let us remember they were tricked by the master trickster, satan himself.

They paid a price that took them to a place I would say they never desired to go. Some have been taken out the game for legal reasons while some by way of death. Two were taken as a result of premature death that we look at and two medical deaths.

While we see the body leave this earth, there is another dimension that remains forever; it's called the soul. It is the soul that we believe God redeemed; like the thief on the cross they received God's grace and His mercy.

So let's look at our subjects; at what they gave up to get what they got. Then as a result of their end, can anyone say it was totally worth it? I am not saying their lives were not worth it, I am asking did the price they ultimately paid honor them, their gift or the gift giver. God has a plan for each of us; it is up to us to use our God-given gifts according to His plan and His purpose. If we do that we can live long, success filled lives. Let's start with a well known artist from my father's generation.

My Father's Generation - Sam Cooke:

Samuel Cook, (January 22, 1931 - December 11, 1964), better known under the stage name Sam Cooke, an African American gospel, R&B, soul, and pop singer, songwriter, and entrepreneur. This is a resume second to none. Sam Cooke was born in Chicago, Illinois. He was one of eight children of Charles Cook Sr., a Baptist minister; A PK. When Sam sang as a little boy in church, everyone made note that his voice had "something special". He sang in church and in local gospel choirs until a group called the Highway Q.C.'s asked him to sing with them. By the time he reached 20, Sam's voice was a finely honed instrument and he was noted for bringing the spirit up in churchgoers. In other words he was highly gifted.

When Sam replaced R.H. Harris, the legendary lead singer for the extremely popular gospel group The Soul Stirrers, it was the beginning of his meteoric rise. Cooke sang with the group for six years, traveling back and forth across the country and gaining a wealth of knowledge regarding how black people were truly treated. His refusal to sing at a segregated concert led to what many have described as one of the first real efforts in civil disobedience and helped usher in the new Civil Rights Movement. He refused to be exploited.

After several gospel albums, Sam decided it was time to cross over from gospel (against almost everyone's advice) to record some soul and rhythm & blues. His hypnotically smooth voice, not to mention his finely chiseled good looks, brought him almost instant success.

His first single released in 1957 was "You Send Me", which sold over a million copies and made Sam an "overnight success" in the business. He was on his way to becoming the biggest voice on the radio. Record producers vied to sign him to a contract. The record companies recognized the wealth they could acquire using Sam's talents.

In 1960 he became the first major black artist to sign with RCA Records. However, Sam was smart. It did not take him long to realize he could take control. Sam was not happy with the deal and when the time was right decided to start his own publishing company (KAGS Music) to keep control over his music and his own record company (SAR/Derby) to keep control of his money.

He is considered to be one of the pioneers and founders of soul music. He is commonly known as the King of Soul for his distinctive vocal abilities and influence on the modern world of music. His contribution in pioneering Soul music led to the rise of Aretha Franklin, Bobby Womack, Al Green, Curtis Mayfield, Stevie Wonder, Marvin Gaye, and popularized the likes of Otis Redding and James Brown. He had one flaw that the devil was aware of that would cause his ultimate fall.

Sam had 29 top 40 hits in the U.S. between 1957 and 1964. Major hits like "You Send Me", "A Change Is Gonna Come", "Cupid", "Chain Gang", "Wonderful World", and "Twistin' the Night Away" are some of his most popular songs. Cooke was also among the first modern black performers and composers to attend to the business side of his musical career. He founded both a record label and a publishing company as an extension of his careers as a singer and composer. He also took an active part in the Civil Rights Movement.

Sam married his high school sweetheart, Barbara Campbell, in 1959 and they had three children. Tragically, their youngest child, Vincent, drowned in their swimming pool at age four in June 1964.

On the night of December 11, 1964, Sam had withdrawn some money to buy Christmas presents. The manager of the motel he was staying in, Bertha Franklin, who had shot and killed a man six months previously at the same motel, made arrangements with a local prostitute named Elisa Boyer to pick up Sam at a local bar and bring him back to the motel. As he and the woman entered the motel room Sam was struck on the head and momentarily knocked out. Boyer, who was known as a "drunk-roller" who would rob her clients, took Sam's money and met Franklin at the motel office.

When Cooke regained consciousness he was disoriented, in addition to being without his pants and his wallet. He stumbled to the motel office and saw Boyer and Franklin counting his money ($2,500 - a considerable amount of money at the time) through the window. He demanded his pants, money and wallet back. When they didn't open the door, Cooke knocked on it as hard as he could and it came off the hinges. When he got up off the floor Mrs. Franklin shot him and then instructed Boyer to run down the street and call for the police from a phone booth. Boyer told them a phony story about a rape and left the scene and subsequently disappeared. Sam was dead when the police arrived and, since Boyer had stolen his wallet, they had no idea who it was and took it as a routine justified homicide. To the police Sam was just another dead black man.

The coroner's inquest should have been a slam-dunk, but not one pertinent question was asked by an investigator, nor was a background check made that would have revealed Bertha Franklin's deadly past. The authorities simply took her made-up story as "gospel". Sam's murder was chalked up as just another unidentified "rapist" killed in Watts; California justice. It wasn't until the following Monday morning that a reporter found out Sam Cooke was signed in to the motel registry as himself and that one of the world's greatest talents and a true human being was dead, under shady circumstances that might never be covered by the media. At the time, the courts ruled that Cooke was drunk and distressed, and that the manager had killed Cooke in what was later ruled a justifiable homicide.

Sam Cooke was becoming a powerful figure not just on the music scene, but on the business side of the industry as well. His refusal to succumb to outside influences had become career-threatening, and behind-the-scene factors concerning his death have been written about extensively in a biography from his family's perspective. The devil will destroy you if you are not careful. Sam was the son of a preacher, a "PK". His gift had made room for him, but his character had caused him his life. Another tragic loss! He used his God given-talents in church; there was no monetary gain in the church. However, he soon found fame and fortune in the world. The gospel industry does not support its own as the secular world supports. As a gospel singer he was famous, but he was tired and broke. As a secular artist he gained both fame and fortune. The devil set a trap for him, one he never saw coming.

What is not mentioned is how this woman knew he had cash on him? How did the woman in the motel know he had gone to the bank, and how much money he had available in his pockets? The devil set his trap, and carried out his scheme; as a result another life lost.

Sam Cooke's extraordinary musical genius was offset by the flaw of being a serial skirt-chaser and philanderer. It was his wandering eye that led him to his death. In the spirit realm his condition is known as the lust of the eyes. Young men be careful, this has caused many to fall. But God is just and faithful to forgive. We are in no position to say he was lost; what we can say is had he not been an easy mark, he may still be here today.

My Generation - Teddy Pendergrass

Theodore DeReese "Teddy" Pendergrass (March 26, 1950 - January 13, 2010) was an American R&B/soul singer and songwriter. Pendergrass first rose to fame as lead singer of Harold Melvin & the Blue Notes in the 1970s before a successful solo career at the end of the decade. In 1982, he was severely injured in an auto accident in Philadelphia, resulting in his being paralyzed from the waist down. After his injury, he founded the Teddy Pendergrass Alliance, a foundation that helps those with spinal cord injuries. Pendergrass commemorated 25 years of living after his spinal cord injury with star filled event, 'Teddy 25 - A Celebration of Life' at Philadelphia's Kimmel Center. His last performance was on a PBS special at Atlantic City's Borgata Casino in November 2008.

Pendergrass had four children, Tisha, LaDonna, Tamon and Teddy II. In 1987, he married a former Philadanco dancer named Karen Still, who had also danced in his shows. Karen was Pendergrass' primary caregiver. The couple amicably divorced in 2003. Pendergrass met Joan Williams in the spring of 2006. Pendergrass proposed to Joan after four months and they married in a private ceremony officiated by his Pastor Allyn Waller of Enon Tabernacle Baptist Church on Easter Sunday, March 23, 2008. A formal wedding was celebrated at The Ocean Cliff Resort in Newport, Rhode Island on September 6, 2008.

Pendergrass was born Theodore DeReese Pendergrass at Thomas Jefferson Hospital in Philadelphia, Pennsylvania.

He was the only child of Jesse Pendergrass and Ida Geraldine Epps. Teddy was an extremely gifted child, blessed by God with the gift of music. His relationship with God truly began in his mother's womb. God knew us before we were even born. At the tender age of two his mother would stand him on a chair in church and he would sing praises to the Lord. He dreamed of being a pastor and got his wish; at 10, he was ordained a minister. Pendergrass grew up in Philadelphia and sang often at church. When Pendergrass was still very young, his father left the family; Jesse Pendergrass was murdered when Teddy was 12. He also took up drums during this time and was a junior deacon of his church. Pendergrass attended Thomas Edison High School for Boys in North Philadelphia (now closed). He sang with the Edison Mastersingers. He dropped out in the eleventh grade to enter the music business, recording his first song "Angel With Muddy Feet." That recording, however, was not a commercial success. The trap was set. Pendergrass played drums for several local Philadelphia bands, eventually becoming the drummer of The Cadillacs. In 1970, the singer was spotted by the Blue Notes' founder, Harold Melvin (1939-1997), who convinced Pendergrass to play drums in the group. However, during a performance, Pendergrass began singing along, and Melvin, impressed by his vocals, made him the lead singer; his gift made room for him. Before Pendergrass joined the group, the Blue Notes had struggled to find success. That all changed when they landed a recording deal with Philadelphia International Records in 1971. That was the beginning of Pendergrass's successful collaboration with label founders Kenny Gamble and Leon Huff.

In 1972, Harold Melvin and the Blue Notes released their first single, a slow, solemn ballad titled "I Miss You". The song was originally written for the Dells, but the group passed on it. Noting how Pendergrass sounded like Dells lead singer Marvin Junior, Kenny Gamble decided to build the song with Pendergrass.

He was 21 at the time of the recording. Pendergrass sings much of the song in a raspy baritone wail that would become his trademark. The song also featured Blue Notes member Lloyd Parks singing falsetto in the background and spotlighted Harold Melvin adding in a rap near the end of the song as Pendergrass kept singing. The song, one of Gamble and Huff's most creative productions, became a major rhythm and blues hit and put the Blue Notes on the map.

The group's follow-up single, "If You Don't Know Me by Now", brought the group to the mainstream with the song reaching the top ten of the Billboard Hot 100 while also reaching number-one on the soul singles chart. Like "I Miss You" before it, the song was originally intended for a different artist, fellow Philadelphian native Patti LaBelle and her group Labelle but the group could not record it due to scheduling conflicts. Pendergrass and LaBelle developed a close friendship that would last until Pendergrass' death. The group rode to fame with several more releases over the years including "The Love I Lost", a song which predated the upcoming disco music scene; the ballad "Hope

That We Can Be Together Soon", and socially conscious singles "Wake Up Everybody" and "Bad Luck", the latter song about the Watergate scandal.

One of the group's important singles was their original version of the Philly soul classic, "Don't Leave Me This Way", which turned into a disco smash when Motown artist Thelma Houston released her version in 1976.

By 1975, Pendergrass and Harold Melvin were at odds, mainly over monetary issues and personality conflicts. Despite the fact that Pendergrass sung all of the group's songs, Melvin was controlling the group's finances.

Pendergrass left the group in 1977 and the Blue Notes struggled with his replacements. They eventually left Philadelphia International; by the early 1980s had disbanded for good. In 1977, Pendergrass released his self-titled album, which went platinum on the strength of the disco hit, "I Don't Love You Anymore".

Its follow-up single, "The Whole Town's Laughing At Me", became a top 20 R&B hit. It was quickly followed by Life Is a Song Worth Singing, in 1978. That album was even more successful with its singles including "Only You" and "Close the Door". The disco single, "Get Up, Get Down, Get Funky, Get Loose" was popular in dance clubs. The year 1979 brought two successes, Teddy and the live release, *Live Coast to Coast*. Hits off *Teddy* included "Come and Go With Me" and "Turn Off the Lights". His 1980 album, *TP*, included his signature song, "Love TKO" and the Ashford & Simpson composition, "Is It Still Good to You".

Between 1977 and 1981, Pendergrass landed five consecutive platinum albums, which was a then-record setting number for a rhythm and blues artist. Pendergrass' popularity became massive at the end of 1977. With sold-out audiences packing his shows, Pendergrass' manager soon noticed that a huge number of his audience consisted of women of all races. They devised a plan for Pendergrass' next tour to play to just female audiences, starting a trend that continues today called "women's only concerts". At his concerts for women, audience members were given chocolate teddy bear-shaped lollipops to lick. In later years, Mr. Pendergrass would say he was slightly embarrassed by those shows.

"As outgoing as I am, I'm still a country boy," he told The Philadelphia Inquirer in 2002. "It was complimentary, but it was also hard to handle."

With five platinum albums and two gold albums, Pendergrass was on his way to be what the media was calling him, "the black Elvis", not only in terms of his crossover popularity but also due to him buying a mansion akin to Elvis' Graceland, located just outside of his hometown of Philadelphia. By early 1982, Pendergrass was the leading R&B male artist of his day usurping competition including closest rivals Marvin Gaye and Barry White. In 1980, the Isley Brothers released "Don't Say Goodnight (It's Time for Love)" to compete with Pendergrass' "Turn Off the Lights", which sensed Pendergrass' influence on the quiet storm format of black music.

On March 18, 1982, in the East Falls section of Philadelphia on Lincoln Drive near Rittenhouse Street, Pendergrass was involved in an automobile accident. The brakes failed on his 1981 Rolls-Royce Silver Spirit, causing the car to hit a guard rail, cross into the opposite traffic lane, and hit two trees. Pendergrass and his passenger, Tenika Watson, a nightclub performer with whom Pendergrass was acquainted, were trapped in the wreckage for 45 minutes. While Watson walked away from the accident with minor injuries, Pendergrass suffered a spinal cord injury, leaving him paralyzed from the waist down.

In August 1982, his label released *This One's for You*, which failed to chart successfully, as did 1983's *Heaven Only Knows*. Both albums included material Pendergrass had recorded prior to his accident. The albums completed Pendergrass' contract with Philadelphia International, in which by that time Pendergrass decided to return to the studio to work on new music and struggled to find a recording deal.

Eventually signing a deal and completing physical therapy, Pendergrass released Love Language in 1984. The album included the pop ballad "Hold Me", featuring a then unknown Whitney Houston.

Pendergrass became an advocate for people with spinal cord injuries, forming the Teddy Pendergrass Alliance, a nonprofit group, in 1998 to help them. In 2007, 25 years after his accident, he appeared at "Teddy at 25: A Celebration of Life, Hope and Possibilities," a benefit concert for the group in Philadelphia.

On June 5, 2009, Pendergrass underwent successful surgery for colon cancer and recovered to return home. A few weeks later he returned to the hospital with respiratory issues. After seven months, he died of respiratory failure on January 13, 2010, at age 59 with wife Joan by his side, while hospitalized at Bryn Mawr Hospital in suburban Philadelphia.

Pendergrass was a talented big hearted man with a condition that caused him his freedom of movement as well as his reputation; the lust of the eye. The devil managed to knock him off his square by luring him into an immoral relationship that ended with him being paralyzed. What is not mentioned is his amazing love for his children, his mother as well as his continued devotion to God.

When he made his transition he seemed to have returned to the will of God. He had returned to his first love, the church. Remember, as a child before he knew anything else, he was singing praises to God. Here again, did the church turn their backs on him and his gift, causing him to use his talents in other area? Many artist love God, and sing love songs, and other genres of music because the 'saints' "buy and copy". What do I mean buy and copy; one will buy it and allow all their friends, choir members and church sisters and brothers to make copies. However, those in the secular world buy and will allow you to listen. I have found with R&B listeners you have to buy your own. Like so many men in the music business Teddy seemed, from all accounts, to be searching for the love he sang about. He appeared to have the absolute love of his family, but what about the intimate love he sought?

His multiple marriages were an indicator that something was missing. Again, God is not short on forgiveness. Teddy's return to God was an indicator that he loved the Father, and what loving father turns their back on a child when they return home? The prodigal son is an example for us to use as a demonstration of God's love, even when we fall.

Our Children's Generation - Great Beyond Her Time - Whitney Houston:

Whitney Elizabeth Houston (August 9, 1963 - February 11, 2012) Whitney Houston was born in what was then a middle-income neighborhood in Newark, New Jersey, the second child of Army serviceman and entertainment executive John Russell Houston, Jr., *and gospel singer. She was of* African American, Native American and Dutch descent. Her mother, along with cousins Dionne Warwick and Dee Dee Warwick, godmother Darlene Love and honorary aunt Aretha Franklin were all notable figures in the gospel, rhythm and blues, pop, and soul genres. She met her honorary aunt at age 8, or 9, when her mother took her to a recording studio. Houston was raised a Baptist, but was also exposed to the Pentecostal church. After the 1967 Newark riots, the family moved to a middle-class area in East Orange, New Jersey, when she was four.

At the age of 11, Houston began to follow in her mother's footsteps and started performing as a soloist in the junior choir at the New Hope Baptist Church in Newark, where she also learned to play the piano. Her first solo performance in the church was "Guide Me, O Thou Great Jehovah". When Houston was a teenager, she attended Mount Saint Dominic Academy, a Catholic girls' high school in Caldwell, New Jersey, where she met her best friend Robyn Crawford, whom she described as the "sister she never had". While Houston was still in school, her mother continued to teach her how to sing in addition to her mother, Franklin, and Warwick.

Houston was also exposed to the music of Chaka Khan, Gladys Knight, and Roberta Flack, most of whom would have an impact on her as a singer and performer.

This was the beginning of the hype. Whitney an American recording artist, actress, producer, and model was cited in 2009, by Guinness World Records as the most-awarded female act of all-time. Houston was also one of the world's best-selling music artists, having sold over 170 million albums, singles and videos worldwide. She released seven studio albums and three movie soundtrack albums, all of which have diamond, multi-platinum, platinum or gold certification. Houston's crossover appeal on the popular music charts, as well as her prominence on MTV, starting with her video for "How Will I Know", influenced several African-American female artists to follow in her footsteps.

Houston is the only artist to chart seven consecutive No. 1 Billboard Hot 100 hits. She is the second artist behind Elton John and the only female artist to have two number-one Billboard 200 Album awards (formerly "Top Pop Album") on the Billboard magazine year-end charts. Houston's 1985 debut album Whitney Houston became the best-selling debut album by a female artist at the time of its release.

The album was named *Rolling Stone*'s best album of 1986, and was ranked at number 254 on *Rolling Stone*'s list of the 500 Greatest Albums of All Time. Her second studio album Whitney (1987) became the first album by a female artist to debut at number one on the *Billboard* 200 albums chart.

Houston's first acting role was as the star of the feature film The Bodyguard (1992). The film's original soundtrack won the 1994 Grammy Award for Album of the Year.

Its lead single, "I Will Always Love You" became the best-selling single by a female artist in music history. With the album, Houston became the first artist (solo or group, male or female) to sell more than a million copies of an album within a single week period under Nielsen SoundScan system. The album makes her the top female act in the top 10 list of the best-selling albums of all time, at number four. Houston continued to star in movies and contribute to their soundtracks, including the films Waiting to Exhale (1995) and The Preacher's Wife (1996). The Preacher's Wife soundtrack became the best-selling gospel album in history. This was a true tribute to her beginnings.

On February 11, 2012, Houston was found dead in her guest room at the Beverly Hilton Hotel, in Beverly Hills, California, of causes not immediately known. However, The Los Angeles County coroner's office later determined that Whitney Houston's official cause of death is: "drowning and effects of atherosclerotic heart disease and cocaine use." Whitney was making a change; she appeared to be returning to her roots. "I Look to You" is a clear indication that she was once again looking to the Father for strength and guidance. The devil had a trap for her that weekend. She was afraid, lost and even though she had a room full of people around her she was alone.

Since life and death is the Lord's I feel the Lord said enough is enough; Whitney come on home. You have been deceived long enough. Some that knew her personally have stated after her transition; "Looking back, it seemed all she wanted was acceptance and love." Kevin Costner stated this best at Whitney's life celebration. You are most likely thinking she had a lot of love, but there is a level of love that we sometimes need that goes beyond a family member or a friend. Even in her selection of friends, Whitney was not without criticism. Those on the outside looking in had no idea what it is like to constantly feel you are not good enough.

Much like Sam, Whitney made her transition outside the arms of those she held dearest in her heart. With so many people in her inner-court she still left like so many others before, alone.

She wasn't in a hospital, nor was there a doctor at her side, she was alone. The hype, the deception, the fear and the loneliness all over; her gift had taken her to record breaking heights, yet they could not prevent her from making her transition at such an early age. That evening of her transition it appears she was looking for that final acceptance from the very ones she had made so much possible. Rest in peace Whitney, you deserve it. Her final dependence was in God.

They were CAUGHT UP IN THE HYPE!

Everyone desires to have their talents spotlighted, especially if they are gifted and feel they have something to offer. The devil's job has always and continues to be to trick and deceive the very elect of God.

Remember when Christ was sent into the wilderness? The bible says He was tempted of the devil. Had Jesus not known the word He too, may have been caught up in the hype the devil presented! What hype? Look at what he, satan presented to Christ. (Matt 4:1-10.) Then Jesus was led by the Spirit into the wilderness to be tempted by the devil. After fasting forty days and forty nights, he was hungry. The tempter came to him and said, "If you are the Son of God, tell these stones to become bread." Jesus answered, "It is written: 'Man shall not live on bread alone, but on every word that comes from the mouth of God."
Then the devil took him to the holy city and had him stand on the highest point of the temple. "If you are the Son of God," he said, "throw yourself down. For it is written: "'He will command his angels concerning you, and they will lift you up in their hands, so that you will not strike your foot against a stone." Jesus answered him, "It is also written: 'Do not put the Lord your God to the test." Again, the devil took him to a very high mountain and showed him all the kingdoms of the world and their splendor. "All this I will give you," he said, "if you will bow down and worship me." Jesus said to him, "Away from me, satan! For it is written: 'Worship the Lord your God, and serve him only." After Christ had fasted for forty days the devil sat out to trick and trap Christ.

Satan tried on three separate times to get Christ to forsake His purpose and His destiny. After Christ withstood the test satan departed and God sent angels to minister to Christ.

What does that tell you? For me it meant if we allow our God given gifts to stand for God's intended purpose, we will be tested. We will be challenged. We will be presented with situations that make the trap seem like a gift; a blessing.

However, when we fail to step back and examine what we are presented with from a spiritual perspective then like these jewels we will fall. And we will never know if God got His glory?

Who are we to say that either of them was eternally lost; the thief on the cross was saved just at the point of death. Are we to make assumptions based on what we believe should have been done. I will say this; Sam, Teddy and Whitney, being who they were in the Lord were believers. Whitney, loved the Lord, and it was so obvious when she sang songs of Zion. We may be saved in the end, but will we receive our total, eternal reward?

I recently heard a statement made by my Pastor. He stated in part; "When I get to heaven, and stand before Jesus (God) I want to be able to say, that I used everything; gifts you gave me, not just used them but used them up." How profound is that? To be able to state with joy and with godly assurance that I stand knowing that I did run well!

There are many, many more gifted singers, musicians, athletes and artist besides these I could have chosen with abilities that reach far beyond gifted and talented.

Who like these have made their transitions without fully understanding their promise, or destiny? Very few people ever reach their God given potential, me included. Take me; I fight the spirit of procrastination.

For years I never knew there was such a thing. Lack of knowledge can cause us to lose as much as those that may have a drinking disorder, or someone who fights the lust of their flesh.

I just thought "Tomorrow" was an acceptable response to not completing an assignment had I put forth the effort, I could have finished today. Now that I know and recognize what it is I am struggling with, I fight daily to live up to my God given abilities. I ask myself constantly, if what I am doing is getting me closer to my destiny?

Will what I am doing help me to reach my goal? After spending thousands of dollars on trainings and seminars, I came back with the same questions. How ironic is that? I am not bashing these models; what I am attempting to do is demonstrate through what they have publicly shared and how their lives have ended, that we need to guard our children; their gifts and their hearts; don't be afraid to stand your ground and believe God for what is best for them and us. Saying "no" is not a sin; and it does not stop us from becoming who and what God has ordained us to become. Perhaps saying no, could make available the doors to other avenues and opportunities.

We must believe that we have a sure destiny. God did not say He might have a future for us, He allowed us the test for a testimony. He allows us to go through so that we can know beyond a shadow of a doubt that He will never leave us nor forsake us.

When I was around 12 I was molested by my several family members. It was also during this time in my life that I sought God and found Him. One night after one of the violators left my room; I was lying there crying when my room got bright like someone had turned on a light. When I looked up I saw a man hovering over my bed; only I wasn't afraid. There was a peace in that room, I can still sense to this day. I knew it was a man from the voice, not because I saw his face, it was his voice.

He spoke to me in a still quiet voice; "Do not be afraid." At this point in my life I felt alone and not sure of my purpose for being alive. I had spent 8 months with my mother, during which time I had experienced mostly evil. By this time for a strange man to be in my room to me was better than those that were there in the house with me. I just wanted to go back home to my father's house; the abuse I experienced being at my mother's house was not experienced there. My very presence there at my mother's was brought about by deception. My destiny was put on hold. Here, I was no longer the student that competed to be first, here it didn't matter. Here, I had no one telling me I was special, I was there for one reason only. My mother had started another family, and she was in need of a babysitter. I was of age, and was cheap (free).

These things I am sharing with you to serve as an example of how satan can trick you, me or anyone who God has ordained for greatness. Not knowing what to do, I hid myself in the covers of books. I became the lovely people I read about on the pages of the hundreds of books I turned to for comfort.

When I finally returned to my father's house, only one person recognized me being different. She asked the question right out, and my silence gave her the answer. My mother gave birth to me. However, beyond that; she left me with my father and his mother. As a result of the incest, molestation and rape, I saw myself as good for only one thing. I valued myself as worthless. No one cared, so I stopped caring as well. If I had been able to see beyond the events taking place in my life, I would have been able to recognize God's hand in things. I would have been able to reach my God-given potential sooner. Women, who were considered loose, when I was younger, were labeled in the worst way, which is what I saw myself as. In my sight I was without hope. But God knew me and knew that day was coming before the foundation of the world was formed. God took a wretch like me and cleaned me up; let me know that I was loved.

I knew my future was bleak and without hope. However, what I did not see is God was in control. God knew when He chose who my parents would be who I was destined to become if I followed Him.

They were DECEIVED!

These are examples of just a few of the many world famous personalities who were honoring God with their gift of song, singing songs of praises when they were sought out. They were then lured by deceivers by the promise of better; a better lifestyle; more money and fame. Isn't it ironic how the world has to come to the house of God in search of its most gifted to make their money? The dollar is the trap that is used to persuade innocent, gifted and most often anointed minstrels. What we fail to remember is satan headed the music department at the time of his fall. He was not the ugly creature we see portrayed today. Satan was adorned and was said to be the most gifted of God's heavenly angels. He was not the long eared, long tail creature depicted; no he was said to be beautiful. It is amazing we have been granted something the angels do not possess, "A free will", therefore, satan must seek permission from God to go after those he is seeking to devour. (Job 2) He is said to work in the children of disobedience. Wow. So are we to believe that these gifted people were all children of disobedience or tricked? I rather believe they were tricked. They were tricked into believing that the answer to all their problems would be found in the amount of money they would make if only............

The bible ask a profound question in that it request us to think about what our end will be if we gain the whole world and lose our souls? (Matt 16:26) That is such a simple question, yet few, if any really give it real thought.

Bill Withers stated in a documentary about his life and career, that because the music industry is filled with so many dishonest people, he made his decision to get out.

But what he has not given up on is his music. He continues to be the music minstrel he was designed to be; only he does it on his own terms not on the terms of tricksters and greedy promoters.

Like a horse is drawn away by the possibility of chewing on a crisp carrot, young gifted youth are lured into an industry that promises stardom, riches and fame. They receive everything promised, and more. "The more" is the part they are not prepared to handle. What isn't told to these up coming stars are the prices they will have to pay to obtain their so-called fame. They are not told they will have to make sacrifices they are unprepared to make. They will have to give up other dreams and desires that in some cases they were already prepared to work to achieve. They aren't told that beneath all the hype and the promises of stardom and success they would have to suffer. They are unprepared and in many cases they turn to what is conveniently laid out before them; drugs and alcohol.

Fame was found at a higher price than they had imagined; selling out their self respect and moral values. The very essence of who they were is lost in the thick of ideals they are fed in their quest to become who someone else has filled their minds and hearts with who they can be.
Imagine someone walking up to you and telling you in a rhetorical way;

"did you know that you are a girl or boy whatever the case may be" as if you did not know, and you

accept their statement as new found knowledge!! Then you are promised a life and a lifestyle you are not prepared to live. This is what happened to these talented men and women. As a result, they become troubled, mean, insecure and ultimately the demands on them and their life caused them to become self destructive. The sad thing is many of them never stop to see or realize when destruction takes a friend that same destruction can also destroy them. Each time a star fall heaven weeps. Heaven weeps because we are given free will; but we choose to go the way that is opposite of us getting to God. The word of God states when we know to do right and does not it is sin. (James 4:17) What a gift life is to those who stay the course! You've heard, of course, of Job's staying power, and you know how God brought it all together for him at the end.

(Job 42:12) That's because God cares, cares right down to the last detail. (James 5:11b- MSG) As we look into the lives of each of these talented young former Christians we see that those who were supposed to cover them did not appear to be clear about their role in their lives.

They allowed others to take over; both the gift and the child. Of all the people who were in the lives of our subjects, couldn't anyone see that the gift and the gifted were being removed from God? Let's take a look at who their covering may have consisted of: their pastors, parents and friends.

Will their pastor as their spiritual leader be held accountable if he failed to heed a word of warning to that sheep? If mom and dad were Christians, will they also be held accountable? There are also the family and friends who looked at the material advantages who may have known better, will they be held accountable as well? Are we so blinded by material gains that we forget about our place in God? I believe those who were chosen as coverings will be held accountable in the end. But who am I to say, they have not sought God for themselves in an effort to seek His forgiveness for not living up to the position He gave them to fill. I believe those that have been left behind now have to face their loss and are forced to suffer greater than the person they have lost.

They now have to live out their days in if only I would 'a, could' a or should' a. In the end God alone knows. Is the wealth left behind enough to replace the loss of the person? Is their remembrance enough? Again these are questions only they can answer. Sometimes there are those who got caught up in the glamour of the industry who returns to their first love, before they come to their end.

Sometimes we come to our senses then realize God is not pleased with the life that we lead and we listen and obey when he calls us back. When we obey His voice we are blessed to receive His over-flow blessings. Keep in mind; our mess and misuse of our gifts blocks God's complete blessings in our lives. Failing to heed God's warnings because we listen more to man; out of our fear of rejection, is far worse than any failure or rejection caused by man.

God is a faithful God. He is a jealous God as well. He has every intention of bringing to pass His promises He has placed in our heart.

So why do we turn to man to aide God: because time is the enemy of faith? In our impatience we fail to see that God has His own timing for all things, as a result we tend to be like Sarah.

When God promised He would make Abraham the father of nations, Sarah thought she needed to help God; as a result she made a mess of the future of her nation.

God said He would supply all our needs: that He would make room for our gifs, yet we often turn to man who prospers as a result of our gift, and then have us wait on the side when our usefulness to them has passed, as they bait their hooks for others to prey. I admire artist who work hard to achieve their dreams; and through the grace of God they achieve God's blessings as a result of their gifts.

There are some famous people; artists, writers, musicians, and play-write who have not completely sold out; as a result many are blessed beyond what they could imagine or even think. Do they keep and hoard their blessing? Nope!

They are givers. It seems the more they give the more returns back to them. Why? Because no man can beat God giving!

On the other hand, fear of rejection will cause us to sit still when we should be moving forward. The unfaithful servant is a biblical example of what fear will cost us.

That servant should have been working, so that he could gain. Instead, he sat and did nothing. When his master returned because he had not worked, he had nothing to show or give beyond what he started with. Out of fear when he was given a position to fill, he hid his substance. He admitted to his master, because the master was a man to be feared and he was unsure of how to increase what he had been given he did nothing. All that did was get him the thing he feared; which was rejection. God is faithful and just. That means if He has given us a gift, He knows when we are mature enough to handle the gift as well as the blessings which come as a result of the gift. If we on the other hand decide to allow others to guide us and direct us and aide us before our time in the use of our gift we fail to mature; as a result our blessings can become our curse. Not all of those who are gifted stay outside the will of God. There is one such artist that was at the top of her game, when she decided it was time to quit.

She Too was DECEIVED FOR A WHILE
Dubbed the Queen of Disco – But She Remembered the Lord

Let's take a quick look into the life of another songbird. Donna Summer. LaDonna was born *LaDonna Adrian Gaines* on December 31, 1948 in Boston, Massachusetts to parents Andrew and Mary Gaines, one of seven children. She and her family were raised in the Boston neighborhood of Dorchester. Her father, Andrew Gaines, was a butcher, and her mother Mary, was a schoolteacher. LaDonna's mother later recalled that from the time she could talk, LaDonna would often sing: "She literally loved to sing. She used to go through the house singing, singing. She sang for breakfast, for lunch and for dinner." LaDonna was one of seven children born and raised in Boston's Dorchester neighborhood.

LaDonna's performance debut occurred at church when she was ten years old, when she replaced a vocalist who had failed to show up. Her priest invited the young Gaines to perform, judging from her small frame and speaking voice that she would be an "amusing spectacle", but instead LaDonna recalled a voice older than her years and frame. Donna herself recalled that as she sang, "I started crying, everybody else started crying. It was quite an amazing moment in my life and at some point after I heard my voice came out I felt like God was saying to me 'Donna, you're going to be very, very famous' and I knew from that day on that I would be famous." LaDonna later attended Boston's Jeremiah E. Burke High School, where she performed in school musicals and was considered popular.

She was also something of a troublemaker, skipping home to attend parties, circumventing her parents' strict curfew.

In 1967, just weeks before graduation, LaDonna left for New York where she was a member of the blues-rock band, Crow. After they were passed by every record label, they agreed to break up. LaDonna however, stayed in New York and auditioned for a role in the counterculture musical, Hair. When Melba Moore was cast in the part, LaDonna agreed to take the role in the Munich production of the show. She moved to Munich, Germany after getting her parents' reluctant approval. LaDonna eventually became fluent in German, singing various songs in German.

In 1971, she moved Austria where she met and fell in love with actor Helmuth Sommer while the two were acting in Godspell. In 1973, the couple married and that year LaDonna gave birth to her first child, daughter Mimi Sommer. In 1975, the couple divorced. LaDonna took her husband's last name, translated to English, as her stage name.

In 1978, while working on the hit track, "Heaven Knows" which featured Brooklyn Dreams member Joe "Bean" Esposito on vocals, LaDonna met fellow member Bruce Sudano. Within a few months, LaDonna and Sudano became a couple. They married on July 16, 1980. In 1981, LaDonna gave birth to another daughter (her first child with Sudano), Brooklyn Sudano, named after Sudano's group.

In 1982, LaDonna and Sudano had their second child, Amanda. (Brooklyn would grow up to star in the hit ABC production My Wife and Kids.)

In the mid-1980s, Donna Summers was embroiled in a controversy. She had allegedly made anti-gay remarks regarding the then-relatively new disease, AIDS, which as a result had a significantly negative impact on her career. By this time she a born-again Christian, was alleged to have said that AIDS was a punishment from God for the immoral lifestyles of homosexuals. However, she denied that she had ever made any such comment and, in a letter to the AIDS campaign group ACT UP in 1989, she said that it was "a terrible misunderstanding. I was unknowingly protected by those around me from the bad press and hate letters... If I have caused you pain, forgive me. I did not sit with ill intentions in judgment over your lives." She went on to apologize closing her letter with bible quotes from 1 Corinthians 13 (Though I speak with the tongues of men and of angels, and have not charity, I am become as sounding brass, or a tinkling cymbal.)

In 1995, LaDonna and her family moved from Los Angeles to Nashville, where she took time out from show business to focus on painting, a hobby she began in 1985. Also during 1995, LaDonna's beloved mother, Mary, died of lung cancer. LaDonna died on the morning of May 17, 2012, at her home in Englewood, Florida at the age of 63. She had been diagnosed with lung cancer not related to smoking, reportedly being a non-smoker.

She believed she contracted the illness by inhaling toxic particles following the 9/11 terrorist attacks in New York. LaDonna is survived by her husband Bruce Sudano, their daughters Brooklyn and Amanda, as well as her daughter Mimi from a previous marriage. Her funeral was held in Nashville on May 23, 2012.

What is so amazing Donna Summer had turned back to her beginning early in her career. She was not content with the tricks, traps and schemes the music industry painted in an effort to exploit her talents. God had blessed her as He has so many others with the gift of song, and for a while she allowed the traps of the music industry to lure her into what she believed would be a great avenue to expand her talents; and become the famous person she knew she was destined to become. LaDonna set out to let the world know what she had been gifted to give; her gift of song. What seemed like a great opportunity turned into a nightmare of sort? Donna Summer met the love of her life as a result of being in the music business, but even in that she was not content with man alone, she knew she still needed God, so it was to Him that she returned. In her efforts to be the person she knew she was deep down inside and not the person she often must have found herself being she traveled the world looking for the best place to be herself; to show her talents as she displayed her gift.

However, unlike others before her she was able to recognize that she had a lot more to give than what she was putting out. There was a beautiful soul deep inside her that longed to be what God has ordained her to be.

The bible says train up a child in the way they should go, and when they old, they will not depart from it. (Pro. 22:6) So, Donna returned to her roots, the church.

She was a mother as well as a gifted songstress; above all else she loved God.

Rolling Stones magazine described Donna Summers in this way when she made her transition: Donna Summer was more than one of the disco era's most successful artists. She earned a string of hits throughout the Seventies and Eighties with her innovative songwriting and powerful, sensual voice that has influenced dance music for decades.
 From the rough-and-tumble of "Bad Girls" to the triumphant anthem (and wedding favorite) Last Dance and many moving ballads in between; Donna Summer helped define the magic of the dance floor all over the world. Isn't it amazing that they would list all of her accomplishments and never once mention her return to Christ? Why because like others before and since her transition, the world does not recognize the God presence in us, only those characteristics that make them comfortable. God's presence in your life to the world can be uncomfortable. God, family and career was the order of her lifestyle. She did run well.

CONCLUSION

There are countless other artist who could have been included; famous people; people who are known, who are struggling with not only being themselves they also wrestle with the concept of how others have decided they should use their gifts. It's not just our singers who get tricked; there are also the athletes, musicians and political leaders who also fall as a result of the deceiver. Before the ink dries for some who the Lord has allowed to be blessed the enemy comes into their minds and they are trapped. For some when they have reached a certain social status, they are tricked into thinking they are no longer responsible to their maker for the gifts He grants them. We are all accountable for our stewardship over the gifts and blessings God grants us whether the gift is large or small. Some the enemy tricks into thinking they are no longer a part of Him when they stray. His word declares He will never leave nor forsake us. (Heb 13:5) Therefore He is always present watching, praying, and advising us even though we may ignore His voice. For it is His will that none should perish, that all would have everlasting "good" life. Some will spend eternity in torment. That is not God's will for His children. The thief's purpose is to steal and kill and destroy. My (God's) purpose is to give them/us a rich and satisfying life. (2 Peter 3:9) Do not allow yourself to think for one moment that God's end for us is to have us suffer. Since all good and perfect gifts come from the Lord, think for a moment, why would God decide to give us a mind to make bad decisions concerning His gift? Imagine for a moment, you are a parent; even if you have no children, in this role as a parent telling your child to run and stand in the middle of the street; not a slow county road, but a busy intersection. Now, tell that child to stand there no matter what. That is what the devil does. He sets us up each and every one of us to fail. He paints pictures in our minds of things that are not; like a computer screen saver. A good screen saver can give the illusion of fish swimming right on the screen when in fact there are no fish. The devil tricks us by clouding our thoughts and then giving us illusions of grandeur; when in fact we have not succeeded when our success has been obtained outside the will of God. But God has promised; For I will pour water upon him that is thirsty, and floods upon the dry ground: I will pour my spirit upon thy seed, and my blessing upon your offspring. (Isa. 44:3) All we have to do is abide by the word of God. He is just and faithful. As stated earlier; time is the enemy of faith; which is why we struggle. We struggle because we find it hard to believe that God is causing us to wait. God's delay does not mean denial. We have been lead to believe that if it doesn't happen by this time or by the time something else takes place then we must get out there and make it happen. We spend our wheels in an effort to make it happen; many times wasting precious resources in the process. However, the real question is, are we honestly happy when our blessing manifest if we make it come to pass and not God? How do we view others now? Are we secure in our relationships? Do we seek acceptance in others or do we know who we are, and have confidence in our position? As we mature in our gifts and in our walk with the Lord we must be mindful that God is in control of the final outcomes of life; our decisions and even, here is the most important, our destiny. God knows the plan He has for us. Now that does not single out a race, color or creed, only that God knows the plan He has for "you/us". *For I know the plans I* have for you," declares the LORD, "plans to prosper you and not to harm you, plans to give you hope and a future.

Jeremiah 29:11; (NIV) or if we look at it in the King James version; "For I know the thoughts that I think toward you, saith the LORD, thoughts of peace, and not of evil, to give you an expected end." WOW. Either way it sounds like God's plans for us are filled with great expectations. When we venture off on our own without consulting God we set ourselves up for failure. The scripture states "Acknowledge God in all our ways and He will direct our path." (Prov. 3:6) Do we believe God's word? Or do we see this passage as Old Testament, just another scripture before the promise? Does it mean that when we get ready to make life decisions we should be seeking God for directions? After all God is far too busy to answer our insignificant request. With that thought in mind, which is a trick from the pit, we go out and make a mess of things, and then we turn to God.

We think, we can just go and make this money, or date this guy, or buy this car and go on our way, or do whatever. We think it is not necessary to seek God's directions for simple things. God will answer you if you ask Him what to wear. God will direct our paths if we trust in him. Proverbs tells us that He will make those paths straight if we acknowledge Him in all our ways. (Prov. 3:5-6) While I am not the finished product of what God has ordained me to be, I will share with you that if I had acknowledged God;

allowed Him to lead me and not my flesh, I would be standing in a better place in Him now, rather than warning you of the pitfalls of disobedience; or of the danger of moving in self. No one ever told me even though I was in church the blessings available to me according to the promises and will of God. No one ever told me God had a plan for me. No one ever listed the promises of God that are mine for the asking in faith. It was not told to my generation that God would bless us if we walked up right before Him. No, we were only told of what we should not do. Something like the Jews did with the Gentiles during Paul's ministry. You see the Jews had so many laws they couldn't live up to them themselves; yet they expected the Gentiles to follow them. I was given a whole list of things I should not do, but there was never a reward/blessing attached to my not doing them. So, my desire for the youth today is that they know not only the laws of the land, but the word of God.

God's word is what He expects us all to live up to so that He can bestow upon us the blessings that are available to each of us. We are not just born; we are born with a hope and a promise. (Jer. 1:5) Therefore it is up to each of us to tell our children and our children's children of the hope; of the promise, and of the gifts God has for us. What real father gives rocks for a meal to his hungry children? God is no different. In fact God's love for us sets the standard for us to follow as parents, pastors, teachers and leaders. So let us all acknowledge God as the giver of gifts, in our service, and in our ability to give to others from the abundance of gifts God has made available to us.

The next time we are tempted to take credit for the gifts and blessings we so enjoy, let's pause and remember that it is the Lord who gives. It is easy to think when things are going good it is by our abilities that we achieve success. Not so, God knew before the foundations of the world what we would be, and since He designed us and He is a perfectionist; rest in the comfort and knowledge that God makes no junk; that from our beginning we were destined for greatness.

I had a younger sister who like so many was confused in her walk. As a young teenager, she lost her father in a tragic car accident. She blamed her mother who was driving at the time. My sister spent the remainder of her life striking out in anger. You see her father was her heart. She loved him more than anything or anybody else on earth. As the years passed she birthed three beautiful children of her own which she loved dearly. However, because of the anger she harbored toward her mother, she was self destructive. But God; who is rich in mercy did not allow her to leave this earth before she was redeemed.
I believe ready to meet Him face to face.

Personally I believe although the way in which she made her transition was tragic, God snatched her before the devil had an opportunity to totally destroy her mind and body. God had her soul.

Jesus on the cross is our example of the grace God extends to those that believe, even at the point of death He forgave a thief on the cross.

The thief humbled himself and Jesus let him know he would be with him "that day"; And Jesus said unto him, Verily I say unto you, **Today** shall you be with me in paradise. (Luke 23:43) Because the Lord is no respect of person, I believe my sister joined her heavenly Father at the end of her time here on earth.

The same holds true with Sam Cooke; he may have perished in violence, but his soul returned home. Teddy, like so many others including, Donna Summer remembered their Father. Whitney made her declaration that she looked to God in her final recording "I Look to You". If you have never sat and truly listen to the lyrics, you owe it to yourself to do so.

She had survived a tumultuous marriage, a tremendously successful career, and yet, she was troubled. She knew that in order to have the peace she was seeking she would have to return to the one who had made her very life possible. As we see even in our broken and sometimes destructive states, we are still connected to our Heavenly Father.

Each one of our subjects sang love song; each had a unique gift and style; however, each one of them started with their gifts lifted toward heaven.
Even though they each transitioned in a different way, I believe they each returned home.

In conclusion, although some may not receive their just and complete reward God has prepared for them; if we don't give up and live according to His will and purpose; if we trust Him and believe with all our hearts that Jesus is

Lord we will receive a crown of glory; the adornment on our crown is based on our devotion and our faithfulness to the Father. And let us not be weary in well doing: for in due season we shall reap, if we faint not. (Gal 6:9)

*SIN WILL **TAKE** YOU FARTHER THAN YOU WANT TO GO,*

***KEEP** YOU LONGER THAN YOU WANT TO STAY~*

*AND WILL **COST** YOU MORE THAN YOU WANT TO PAY~~*

SIN COST

About the Author

A. Jean White-Jennings has co-hosted as "Mistress of Ceremony" at events and award shows all across the country – Sacramento California, Dallas Texas, Houston Texas, Cincinnati Ohio, Las Vegas Nevada, Oakland California, Los Angeles California, Seattle Washington, Atlanta Georgia, Kansas City Missouri, Detroit Michigan, Chicago Illinois, Indianapolis Indiana, Brooklyn New York and Nashville Tennessee.

When she talks to you about who she is, she paints a picture of a modest woman who enjoys life and finds joy and pleasure in helping others. The more you talk to her the more you see she is much, much more.

Learn from this dynamic mother, motivator, author, teacher and entrepreneur even when life throws you sour, rank lemons, you can still make and sell lemonade.

Ms. Jennings is a consultant to countless women who have their own life stories to share. As a self published author she learned the need for assistance and welcomes others who may need help to contact her.

Copies of "Hidden Hurts Revealed: Biography of A Woman" her first book, was sold to hundreds of men and women after the book's release in 2008. The original publication was later re-called and re-released in 2010; the sequel is due to hit book store in the spring of 2015.

It is her hope that her current book, 29:11 – Everyone's Foundation for A Success Filled Life will open your mind to what it takes to protect yourself, your children as well as others in your circle when it comes to your God given gifts.

Ms. Jennings is also a certified Travel Consultant; certified in over 25 destinations; including the Caribbean, Destination Wedding Sprcialist, Groups and Cruises.

Ms. Jennings is available for motivational lectures upon request.

Contact Information: Min. A. Jean White Jennings
(773) 319-6347

Hiddenhrtsrevealed@sbcglobal.net

Other Works include: Hidden Hurts Revealed: Biography of A Woman – Currently Available: Amazon.Com – coming to eBook Soon.

www.ingramcontent.com/pod-product-compliance
Lightning Source LLC
Chambersburg PA
CBHW072035060426
42449CB00010BA/2264